Breaking the 90% rule of Startup failure

CONTENT

CONTENT ii

Forward iii

Chapter 1: The entrepreneurial journey: -An introduction 1

Chapter 2: Discovering the problem 7

Chapter 3: Examining startup success factors 10

Chapter 4: Redefining failure 12

Chapter 5: Breaking the 90% role at the initial stage 17

Chapter 6: Breaking the rule in investments: What startups should know 30

Chapter 7: Networking... 44

Conclusion - Thrive 53

Forward

Some of the material in this book draws largely from the works of others especially some of the interviews conducted for Evolve business magazine which have greatly inspired this work.

I owe a debt of ideas to Jeremy Pesner, Dalopo Sanusi Ola, Monica McCoy, Hussein Danesh, Ken Kengatharan, Ganesh J., Alex Mond, Ken Kengatharan, Baybars Altuntas and others who in one way or the other influenced this work.

Chapter 1: The entrepreneurial journey: -An introduction

Globally, Sub Saharan Africa has a population of approximately 1.1 billion people. According to join statistics by the African development bank and IFAD of early November 2016, 75% are less than 35 years. Approximately 350 million of them are between the ages of 15-35, and 10 million+ enter the job market yearly. "The entrepreneurial landscape in sub-Saharan Africa is absolutely excellent," says Mike Herrington, executive director of Global Entrepreneurship Mentor (GEM) and professor at the University of Cape Town in South Africa. GEM assets that, sub-Saharan Africa is the region with by far the highest number of people involved in early-stage entrepreneurial activity. But this is nothing compared to the rest of the world.

According to ILO, trends for Youth report show that, as a result of the above, the global number of unemployed youths is was predicted to reach 71 million in 2017. With a youth population that is expected to double, to over 830 million, by 2050 in the whole continent, Entrepreneurship seems to be the way out.

However, the educational system in most African countries does not directly prepare the youths for the job market, and just an insignificant number of private schools prepare them for entrepreneurship.

The World Bank group in an article titled *innovation and entrepreneurship*; recognizes these two things as building blocks of every competitive and dynamic economy. They argue that, countries with innovative and vibrant entrepreneurship ecosystems tend to witness higher productivity rates, leading to increase economic growth and more robust job creation which are the main path ways through which the poor can escape poverty.

The African Development bank is equally of the opinion that, entrepreneurship is key to African economies and advice governments to integrate it fully into their industrialization strategies (African Economic outlook, 2017). It is against this backdrop that this book was written to serve as a tool for entrepreneurs and entrepreneurship especially in developing economies.

This book in the most part captures the simple ideas and processes that when applied can have measurable impacts on business and the way entrepreneurship is practice

Percentages of start-up failure are generally not very uniform but one thing remains; the fact that a majority of them are bound to fail within their first years. In this book, we have chosen the 90% incident of failure and elaborated ways in which this can be minimized.

We are of the opinion that, if certain stages are respected and steps taken into consideration, more startups will succeed. In fact an earlier study carried out in 2016 for the Start-up compass theory (The Altuntas Start-up compass theory, 2016) proved that this had been applied and results achieved. The paper took into consideration 4 different stages

- Before starting the business
- Starting up the business
- Growing the Business including branding, institutionalization, franchising
- Maturing the business involving leadership and Angel investments

This book is written to serve as a guide to startups and to assist them move from ideation to a full business.

What is a Startup?

Different definitions of startup exist and have often varied from one society to another with everyone trying to coin it to suit their specific context. There has equally been a lot of confusion between startups and small businesses which we hope to clarify before proceeding to the next chapter of the book.

An entrepreneurial venture which is typically a newly emerged business that aims to meet a marketplace need by developing a viable business model around the product, service, process or platform. A startup is usually a company designed to effectively develop and validate a scalable business model (Wikipedia)

According to the small business Association, "in the world of business, the word startup goes beyond a company just getting off the ground. The term startup is also associated with a business that is typically technology oriented and has high growth potential.

A startup is a young company that is just beginning to develop. Startups are usually small and initially financed and operated by a handful of founders or one individual (Investopedia).

A startup is a temporal organization aiming to become a successful company (The Altuntas Start-up compass theory)

Paul Graham the founder of Y combinator defines a startup as, a company designed to grow fast. He further explains that, being newly founded does not in itself make a company a startup. Nor is it necessary for a startup to work on technology, or take a venture funding, or have some sort of "exit". The only essential thing is growth, everything else we associate with startups follows from growth.

Within the context of this book, we will define a startup to be *a business that has a potential to scale, potential to grow very fast and a product, service or process they can sell*

To a large market.

For small businesses, this is not the case as they can produce in one country and sell only in that country or in one town and sell only in that town. That limits their market and therefore makes them more of a small business than a startup. The most important thing to note here is the ability to grow or growth simply put.

The difference therefore is in their growth ability, their market, and their vision (while a small business will look to generate cash instantly, a startup might go through many rounds of funding with a planned budget that doesn't seek profitability for the first few years but instead focus on carving out a brand new Market or to disrupt the industry in question where they

Find themselves.

To better understand what a failed startup is, we will prefer to define a successful one. *A successful startup would be one that actually manages to grow into a company which creates sustainable profit.*

i) Who says good things come easily?

So many people admire entrepreneurs and entrepreneurship but fear to get involved because of the ups and downs that come with being one. However, in my opinion nothing good comes easily to anyone, five continuous years of success might be a result of hard work and series of difficulties encountered in life. So do not be afraid to try it and fail but work harder and learn new ways to achive the same results; even better-innovate.

When asked the secret of his success, the CEO of LinkedIn said "right decisions" some people look at it from this perspective and sometimes get many things wrong when they stop just here so he added that, he could take the right decisions now because of the many wrong decisions he had taken in the past. Therefore, move from your comfort zone, start this new journey with the consciousness that, your chances to succeed depend on so much more than the beautiful idea you have in mind. Let each mistake be a lesson and you will emerge stronger and more successful than you ever imagined.

ii) Why this book was written

This book is about understanding failure, redefining it and using it as a stepping stone. This book is not entirely about failure, we only treat failure as a means to identify the real problem we are out to tackle. The entire concept behind this book is to build a strong entrepreneurial culture aimed at taking economies to the next level. It is intended to serve as a vector for innovative thinking and innovation in the startup milieu especially in Africa.

This book does not pretend to provide an excellent solution to resolve issues around startup failure, but if applied, it will reduce the incident of failure to an acceptable level. It seeks to bring to the mind of entrepreneurs, to create a picture in their mind of some of the mistakes they could have made, are making and will eventually make that will lead to the failure of their startup.

When we fail, people might turn to look at us differently, when our startup fails, we might be tempted to get demoralized. Some successful people when they share their testimonies, we begin to think that fortune smiled on them because it sounds so smooth we begin to wish we were like them. Truth is, there is no such thing as a smooth path to success, there is no such thing as gain without sweat. If you want to make it big and make a difference, be ready to make mistakes and if someone's testimony sounds too smooth, 90% of the times, something is missing.

Therefore, it is important to know that, each failure is a lesson and to pick up the courage to move on till we get there.

iii) What you can learn from this book

In this book, you will learn how to initiate your journey into entrepreneurship from a skeptic to a guru, how to select the best business idea from the many others you might have. How to evaluate it, develop it, expand it, find the right resources for it and to stand out. You will also learn reasons why startups succeed, why they fail, how failure can be avoided, fund raising hacks, team building tips and many things that can help take your business to the next level if applied.

Chapter 2: Discovering the problem

Resolving a problem always starts with identifying it. Any guided action aimed at finding a lasting solution to every issue must always start with identification; of the problem, its root cause, its remote cause and its immediate cause. It is only then we can begin to craft a perfect solution to that problem.

i) Choosing a path

Reading through my LinkedIn wall this morning I stumbled on a post that reminded me of the road I have covered and still plan to cover. Written by a successful lady in the corporate world, her worry was whether or not she should say yes to requests from people who wanted to have coffee with her as a way of learning from her.

I spent hours going through each comment and then I realized that life is all about a simple concept, "we learn from people, we learn from circumstances, we learn from processes, we learn from failure, we learn from experience, we learn from everything". The key word here is FROM. This means there is no self-made person. What you have today has an origin, it is coming from somewhere. If you as much as give back a little of all you get to reach out to others, society will be improved greatly.

I have always felt concerned about what happens to people and the society around me. This sometimes left me feeling weird in the mist of otherwise normal people because these things didn't mean same to them.

As time went on however and the years passed by, I came to the knowledge of one thing; we are all created differently and for different purposes and are all on a different mission. What burdens you is your mission and you do not have to wait till everyone feels same to do something about it.

Then, I started getting closer to entrepreneurs and investors; I started observing and later researching to better understand. All through these years I saw a few things; great ideas looking for an opportunity to shine, great startups seeking endlessly for funds, and that some parts of the world were getting more attention from investors than others.

What crowned it all was the incident of startup failure and statistics that were simply hard to belief. Who will accept the fact that 1 out of every 10 startups succeed? Few people I guess, but these are the hard facts. I set out to find a solution to these in whatever way I could and then I set my target of talking to as many entrepreneurs and investors as possible, sampling their thoughts and understanding the whole system from ideation to Unicorns.

ii) Paving a path

My idea was to talk to many entrepreneurs in developing economies especially the most successful ones to find out the secret to their success but I later extended this idea to include people from everywhere in the world. To achieve this in a more constructive way, I launched my business magazine and started documenting these experiences. Today I must admit I have learnt so much talking to each and every one person I have interviewed for my magazine.

My greatest challenge however still remains, if I identify two CEOs I want to interview for my magazine, one from a developed economy and the other from a developing economy, I have 90% chances to close the interview with the one from the developed economy first and

95% of the time I never succeed in getting the interview done with those from developing economies. This has been my greatest challenge. I meet with so much protocol when dealing with these CEOs that I sometimes prefer to use this time spent on breaking their walls to source people elsewhere with the enthusiasm to share and give back their 1cent to the society.

I have learned from both ends and today am writing this book after going through the same struggle of raising capital for startups I work with, and after feeling the pains and struggles involved in growing a startup and haven't heard and shared the pains of many who put in the same efforts but obtain fewer results.

I finally settled on this point, "the power of the African continent, its future lies in the hands of its people, pull down the walls, reach out and hold the hands of others, mentor someone, create a greater and better version of you in someone, and leave a legacy". Let our sense of community extend from our social life to business and we would have found the key to unlock every potential.

iii) Building

No one person can pretend to have the solution to all the problems startups face. In this book, I will not pretend to offer one either. Neither will I claim to have written all this from my own personal experience. It is a combination of my experiences and those of others shared with me over time, a combination of research and good faith from persons who took out time to share their experiences with me. In this book, you will find key growth hacks which if well applied will go a long way to guarantee the success of your startup. You can fail, but don't be discouraged; failure is a new lesson learnt and another opportunity to initiate a new step in another more advanced way.

Chapter 3: Examining startup success factors

Startup succeed for varied reasons most of which sometimes are dependent on their specific environment and business idea. In this chapter, we will be looking at some of these factors which we have decided to categorize into individual factors on the one hand and external influencing factors on the other hand. These chapter draws largely from *The Altuntas Startup compass theory*

- **Individual characteristics**

If a successful startup is one that moves from a startup to company overtime, then it is important to examine reasons why a few succeed.

Authors	Reasons
Carayannis, Popescu, Sipp and	One's personal motivation and ability to take risk
Vivarelli, 1991	Level of familiarity with the sector
Rauch & Frese, 2000	The need for achievement and control
Cross, 1981	Level of skills
Lloyd &Mason, 1983	Level skill of workers
Storey,1982	Higher level of education to previous managerial
Rose, Kumar & Yen,2006	Entrepreneur's educational level, as well as his/her working experience and familial experience with managing a

Source: Adapted from *The Altuntas Startup compass theory*

- **External influencing factor**

Direct Influence	Indirect influence
Regional innovation networks (Vliamos, Halkos & Tzeremes, 2009)	Location of the market where the startup is developed and entrepreneurial risk-perception affect the investment inflows of a start-up, which in turn will affect its success rate given that if such inflows are small, the business cannot develop further (Psaltopoulos, Stathopoulou and Skoura, 2005)
Local Culture (Carayannis & Campbell, 2009). Research has proven that culture has a direct relationship with business success.	Product adaptability is also another key factor that has affected the growth and expansion of some startups because people take a longer period to text and adopt their products hence ,market penetration is extremely slow
Other Regional characteristics (Audretsch, Thurik, Verheul & Wennekers, 2002). Regions like East Africa with stronger entrepreneurial ecosystems have the tendency to attract more success than those in the CEMAC sub region	Unfair competition especially from, multinational companies in some regions
The idea, the funding, the team and the ground for development (Verbovskii, Poletaev and Chayka, 2014)	

Source: Adapted from *The Altuntas Startup compass theory*

Chapter 4: Redefining failure

i) The basic question (what does failure mean to you?)

"Only those who dare to fail greatly can ever achieve greatly" Robert F. Kennedy

Failure is a word common to all in society. I remember reading a story of a young girl who decided to do a video of what she does to come up with the well packaged products she supplies to her clients; episodes of her sleepless nights and great efforts. This reminded me of the fact that society tends to celebrate the results of our work without in the most parts finding out how we got there. Many people admire success; many entrepreneurs will wish to be like Bill Gates and Steve jobs, they admire Microsoft, Apple and all the great unicorns especially in the Silicon Valley. Sometimes what is not evident is the fact that it took hours of unending work, series of trials, and series of failures to arrive at this end product.

It will of course sound absurd to celebrate failure, but maybe the celebration of failure will create a memorable moment that reminds us always that we have learnt one way we must not go about it next time.

In the entrepreneurial world, people with the greatest success stories equally have remarkable stories of failure. Some are willing to share while others are not. Whatever the case, failure does not define us, it is what we make of it that determines the outcome.

ii) Why People perceive failure differently

While the Cambridge dictionary defines failure as *"the fact of someone or something not succeeding"*, Merriam Webster defines it as *"omission of occurrence or performance; specifically failing to perform a duty or expected action"*

We can go on and on with these definitions, but the point is that, though connoting the same thing, it is perceived differently by individuals, group of individuals and even societies. It has a cultural and contextual perception that undeniably plays a great role in the way people react to it.

In fact, in most societies, failure is interpreted negatively and sometimes becomes a real set back especially for entrepreneurs who usually try new ventures and fail.

Our perception of failure determines what we make of it. Let's look at this, after failing to get the perfect formula for the light bulb 10,000 times, remember what Thomas Edison said, "I have not failed. I've just found 10,000 ways that won't work"; perception, this is what failure is all about. Instead of giving up, he gave himself the 10,001[th] reason to try again and we all know the results. No one deliberately sets out to fail, but when failure comes, we have to find the perfect way to deal with it.

In the words of Jeremy Pesner, "I distinguish between the concept that "I failed" and "there was a failure." I don't do so to remove blame or ignore my own shortcomings, but rather to acknowledge that almost any failure is the product of both my own actions and my current life circumstances and factors. This means that I can take it less personally, and that in the future I can be sure to improve both myself and my environment to ensure I do better. Ultimately, failure is often a signal that something needs to be changed, and if someone is willing and able to confront what that change really is, they'll be primed to do much better in the future".

The truth remains that, in most societies, failure; defined to be the state or condition of not meeting a desirable or intended objective is interpreted negatively.

In the startup world, 9 out of 10 startups fail, this does not mean that it is impossible to succeed and this does not also mean that, after a failed attempt one has to give up.

iii) Why startups fail

In his article on startup failure; *"90% of startups fail: Here's what you need to know about the 10%",* Neil Patel whom the Wall street journal calls a top influencer on the web outlines some of the reasons why startups fail. Among them, he mentions the fact that, they make products that no one wants. In fact as many as 42% of them after failure identified the lack of a market need for their product as a single biggest reason for their failure. He thinks if you are going to spend your time making products, you should also spend your time making sure it's the right product for the right market.

Some fail because they overlook many things and interpret having a strong technical team and a good product will play the trick. But this is wrong because in doing so they often undermine business processes with everyone sticking to their main role. A startup can't segment its responsibilities because responsibilities must overlap at some point to ensure for success.

Some fail because in some cases, the company doesn't grow fast enough to secure more funding and because of that, they fail. Growth; fast growth is what entrepreneurs crave, investors need, and markets want. Rapid growth is the sign of a great idea in a hot market. A startup should not be satisfied with marginal single-digit growth rates after many months of operating. If the growth doesn't happen after a certain amount of time, then the growth will not happen. A company that is not growing is shrinking.

When your startup does not grow fast enough, you can't effectively bypass some of the biggest

Startup killers -losing to the competitors, losing customers, losing personnel, and losing passion.

Some entrepreneurs fail because they do not understand that they must work on their business and not in their business. Getting caught up in the minutiae of presentations, phone calls, meetings, and emails can distract the entrepreneur from the heart of the business.

In addition to all these are some of the things we will discuss in the subsequent chapters.

iv) Maximizing failure

Failure as fatal as it may be seen by others is part of the process to success. The same reasons that account for the failure of some startups are the same reasons others succeed. Let me explain, the important thing in life is; knowing what you must not do especially if you want to stay out of trouble. If you know you really would not love to fail, don't have a deficient team, if you want to succeed, test the market, don't just assume your product is market fit, if you want your processes to improve, be flexible enough to innovate.

You will realize therefore that the things you fail to do that lead to your failure as a startup are the same things that if you concentrate on, your startup will succeed. Running a startup needs every bit of all to succeed, from good leadership to the most basic unit of your product.

Failure therefore is something you can avert if you find yourself in the right environment and then take all other things into consideration.

Chapter 5: Breaking the 90% role at the initial stage

i) Understanding your position

Different people have different motivations and reasons why they will prefer to get involved in a personal venture instead of working for someone. Your motivation or whatever reasons you place at the forefront of your decision to follow this path will greatly determine the outcome of what you do, how you do it and what results you get. Studies in the field of entrepreneurship and small businesses reveal the following categories of people and their motivations to get engaged in what they do. The various categories identified so far are:

Freedom Seekers – These are persons whose primary drive in starting a business in their name is because they want the ability to control their time, fate, decisions, work environment, schedule and revenue. To them, time is valuable and they love to manage it themselves as a means to achieve their set goals.

Passionate Creators – Unlike the freedom seekers, these are people who pursue the entrepreneurial path because they love what they do and the people they serve. Therefore getting involved in what they do gives them a sense of accomplishment and pride. To them, it is more about impact, they value the impact they create in the lives of others.

Skeptics –They love to own their own businesses, they actually own and run them but the real challenges businesses face every day tend to play a lot on them. They have significant concerns, misgivings and skepticism about the value of owning their own business. They tilt towards the reality that, sometimes running a business is more risky than rewarding. Don't get them wrong, they will love to be like every other person doing the same things they do but they can't help acknowledging these realities even more over time.

Legacy Builders – These are the future guys; they believe in making a name, creating a lasting impact and building ventures that live after them. They dream big and they place long term gains above immediate returns. They just don't think like every ordinary person in their field does, they are building a life time dream and this is what drives them daily; a vision of the future.

It is important to identify where you fall as a starting point in every entrepreneurial venture since your drive will determine your outcome. No doubt the entrepreneurial path is tough as seen from the perspective of the skeptic; no doubt 90% of startups fail, but if 10% succeed, then it means your venture can make up part of those who succeed. Start the journey from the origin and let your motivation and your stand be your driving factors.

ii) Tackling the origin-resolving mistakes made from idea conception

After identifying your stand and motivation, the next step is to resolve the problems at the idea conception stage. Whether or not your venture will go pass the first year of operation depends largely on the decisions at the level of conception. This is the reason incubators exist to validate ideas before they are implemented.

This phase is overlooked by many but in essence, it is like the foundation. No one builds a house without a foundation except they are preparing for a suicide mission. If your foundation is strong, then the house will be even stronger and more sustainable.

Before moving from the idea stage to implementation, ask yourself key questions:

- What problem is this product/service going to solve?
- How long will the problem last?
- If the problem ceases to exist tomorrow how can I pivot?
- Which segment of the market am I targeting?
- Why should they be interested in my product?
- Who are my competitors?
- What extra value am I adding?
- What's my MVP?

These and many other questions will determine the future of your venture, they will determine if you get investments and they will determine if you survive market competition. They will equally determine if you move up to the list of the 10% who survive the realities on the market or not, they will determine if you create the impact the passionate creators seek to attend or if you build the future the legacy builders seek to achieve.

Many have said entrepreneurship is an arts, I do not argue this fact, instead I agree with it, let your drawing board be well prepared to host the magnificent panting, let your sculpting tools be well selected to produce a Leonardo da Vinci sculpture.

To make the decision easy for you, let's look at some of the answers to the WH questions in entrepreneurship we mentioned above. As you must already know, it takes more that goodwill and wishes for a business venture to succeed. It takes strategies; the most important one of them being how the venture is managed, who manages it, how it gets it clients, how it maintains client relationship, top management leadership pattern and what have you.

iii) Growing your venture

Getting a good idea is the first step, now that your idea has been validated, what next? You need to be sure that you have the capacity to execute it. If you do not have such, it is important to outsource; staff your weaknesses. This is where your team, board members, advisers, mentors, coaches, resource persons come in. Let's try to give these words some more meaning;

Coaching

Many entrepreneurs overlook the value of coaching probably because they do not know how important it is for their businesses. However, it is important to understand that, because entrepreneurship can often be challenging and even overwhelming, coaching is critical for entrepreneurs, especially for new business owners.

You might be tempted to ask why but this is it; coaches bring wisdom and experience to small business owners that books and blog posts aren't capable of bringing. Don't get me wrong, you can read the books, the articles and the blog post; they have their role to play. But this does not replace the role of a coach who otherwise has lived these experiences, sees the future of your venture and can give you clear pointers on the path to pursue that will lead you to success.

A coach can help an entrepreneur avoid beginner mistakes and grow their business faster than if working alone. Unfortunately, most founders in Africa and some parts of Asia will prefer to try it and fail before getting help the second time. This reduces the incident of success and increases risk of failure which can be avoided at an early stage.

We all know it is easier for others to see our mistakes than for us to realize them on our own; therefore we need that external person who tells us some of the mistakes we are making which could be detrimental to our business in the future. An experienced coach is able to identify shortcomings and avoid major pitfalls, which ultimately allows the entrepreneur to have a more fulfilling business journey. It is therefore highly recommended for business owners to invest in a coach or get someone who is willing to volunteer their time as board member and that can effectively play this role.

Get the right team and board members

Most businesses start up as a one man venture. This can work in small businesses but when it comes to startups, it is detrimental to the future of the startup. A good board of directors; carefully selected is great wealth to the startup especially at its early stage when it has all the management issues. Your board of directors therefore must be solid to accompany you meet the skill set and toolset gapes that exist among founders.

Often times, great business ideas usually emerge from one or more people who are eager to get the idea to the market but do not have what it takes in terms of the skills and tools to ensure its survival in the market. They might however be good in some other aspects. For example, a group of all tech engineers bringing an idea in the market might master the technological part but have knowledge gaps at the level of management, strategy, marketing, fund raising, product management, pitching etc. This is what should guide them in choosing or recruiting their board members.

They should therefore use the recruitment process as a way to staff their weaknesses and make up for all the knowledge and skill gaps.

It is for this reason that, the board of directors must not be selected randomly, otherwise there will not add value to the startup/company. Remember, you can get a high portfolio board member who has the skills you already have or one of your team members already has, this will be a liability rather than an asset to the company. Therefore, the advice is, do not go for the high sounding names and titles if they do not serve a purpose on your board. Rather go for whoever can add value and help push the venture to the next level.

Setting your marketing messages

My intention here is not to treat marketing as a full topic but to point out a few important things that must be considered through the process. Marketing is a very important part of your startups life cycle and should not be overlooked at any point. Having a good business idea is one thing, but getting the right marketing message out is the most important and will determine how many deals you close or how many sales you make.

It is important to remember that, the marketing message is not about you or about the way you perceive your product or service. After all, we all are often times tempted to think our product is the best until it gets to the market. Your message should answer these simple client questions:

What is in it for me? Why should I care?

These two questions otherwise will lead to a single answer that you can use to attract the right target market for your product or service.

Flexibility

The product/service you want to take to the market might be an awesome one. However, you should make sure you only feel wowed by your own product or service after due market research and testing. You might just be surprise that it doesn't really appeal to the market you are targeting. Remember, feeling stuck is something that almost all entrepreneurs go through.

Often times we launch full time into the market without carrying out our research or testing our product and we get stocked. Don't be scared, this can happen to anyone especially if they make the same mistakes you are making. What you need at this point is flexibility; flexibility to think of a different way out, to modify the product or service, to put things right and even to go back to the drawing board-pivoting. In other words you need to be flexible enough to pivot at the right time.

Time

Everything in life needs time to prove itself. Entrepreneurship in the most parts is not for people who do not master the notion of time. Be conscious that your idea needs time to prove itself, your product needs time to conquer the market, your service needs time to gain the confidence of clients, your startup needs time to grow etc.

It is ok to admire the Silicon Valley startups and unicorns, it is ok to admire Apple and Google, and it is ok to admire all the big and famous companies. But remember they needed time to arrive at this point. The long and short of the story is that, entrepreneurship is for those who are patient and who have a vision of the future, a long-term goal and short term strategies to meet the Long term goal. It needs time and you must accept and acknowledge this to stay valid in the Market.

A story is told of a young lady who is taken to a farm with a creeping plant that has produced fruits, some are ready for harvest and others are not. Then she has the liberty to choose any of the fruits that she likes and take home. This is because any fruit she harvests won't impede/affect the continuous growth of the others. This is what happens when you are working for someone that has taken time to build their dreams.

Your input affects the venture as an employee but the success of the venture is not solely dependent on you; the consequences are not directly visible.

In the same light, she is taken to the same farm another season and there is the same creeping plant with same fruits and she proceeds to harvest like the previous season. As she stoops to pick up a fruit, the farm owner immediately warns her of the dangers of picking at random and she is surprise and asks to know why.

The owner explains that, if she happens to pluck the second fruit before the first, she will destroy the first. And so she must proceed in order from the least to the top. This is the secret, you must go progressively in the private venture journey and time must be your guide as every of your actions has a direct consequence on your business.

A child must be conceived, born, nursed, nurtured, must undergo due process to become a man. In all these phases, God's plan for his life is being perfected. Follow God's example and give your business the time it needs to grow because for every investment to be major, it needs time. Businesses need time to grow, networks need time to be established, transactions need time to be concluded etc.

Every good company today just like a child started as an idea, was nurtured, born as a startup, faced all the challenges other startups face. Survived them, grew and today is a big company. Therefore, do not give up just because your business is facing challenges. Let time work for you in your venture.

Time management (refer to Mark smith)

Just like we have seen above, time management is crucial especially for executives. Here our focus will be more on executives because we consider them as the startup engine that generates all the energy which supplies the entire chain. Time obviously has more value than we give it and everyone must be able to manage it well to achieve a work life balance without which, the goal of life is missed.

"A an executive, you are not paid for your hours, you are paid for your outcomes"(Mark Smith)

Mark smith happens to have written some good reflections along this line and we are going to borrow from his advice. He upholds the idea that, an executive's most valuable resource is cognitive capacity. That they are paid because of their ability to create systems, troubleshoot and direct resources to create the outcomes approved by the board of directors. He even breaks it down by stating that, "the bulk of the executive's work is think time and leadership activities not accomplishing specific task"

He seems to focus more of his attention on getting the work done than on how it is done which is a theory upheld by many. We cannot ignore the fact that working flex (flexible) is beginning to heal more results especially in fields that do not really require physical presence to get work done.

Below are the 10 things that are important for executives to know and which Mark Smith titles as, "10 Ways to Get More of What's Important Done"

- Delete from your to-do list the least important thing
- Add a high value goal that you don't yet know how to achieve
- Write the value of accomplishment next to the task
- Always work against a short deadline
- Stop telling others how to do their job and focus on your outcome
- Book time to eat, exercise, and rest
- Schedule an hour for you
- Put reading time on your list – doesn't matter what you read
- Personally celebrate small wins, publicly celebrate big wins
- When you're uncertain what to do, clean your desk and go see a movie.

The above list is aimed at serving as a guide for executives and not a perfect solution to all their problems related to time and outcomes. We therefore intend for them to serve as a guide for you when taking related decisions.

Leadership and processes

The word leadership is one of those words with a thousand definitions that have evolved over time. We will try to bring out a couple of definitions for the purpose of this book.

While the dictionary defines leadership as, the action of leading a group of people or an organization, or the ability to do this and goes a step further to specify that, an effective leader is a person who creates an inspiring vision of the future, motivates and inspires people to engage with that vision, manages delivery of the vision.

Transformational leadership on the other hand sees a leader as someone who coaches and builds a team, so that it is more effective at achieving the vision (transformational leadership).

The business dictionary[1] choses to defines it as;

The act of inspiring subordinates to perform and engage in achieving a goal and its second definition sees it as, the activity of leading a group of people or an organization or the ability to do this.

When we look at some great figures in society, we notice there is equally no unanimity in their definitions.

Peter Drucker defines it as, "The only definition of a leader is someone who has followers."

Bill Gates defines it as, "As we look ahead into the next century, leaders will be those who empower others."

John Maxwell defines it as "Leadership is influence - nothing more, nothing less." Warren Bennis defines it as, "Leadership is the capacity to translate vision into reality." This leaves us with the conclusion that, there is no one size fit all definition for leadership.

---

[1] http://www.businessdictionary.com/definition/leadership.html

As business owners, the temptation to lead at all levels is very high because we are often convinced that we are better placed to handle it all. From the start, this could be easy but as the venture grows, there are things we must take into consideration. In what I chose to title *"The*

Four Jinesh Parekh principles to business success", he advises against the do it yourself style of leadership (DIY).

When we look at the biggest companies in the world, they all practice principles similar to those we will be discussing below. Therefore we can conclude that these principles work.

Building more leaders: The primary job of a leader is to build more leaders who can take over crucial jobs in the company or organization. For this to happen, you must build the company in such a way that it doesn't need you. It should continue executing and growing even if you are gone for a month. This is because you are not perfect at everything so if you can get a team of leaders who are good at other things, they can complement your weaknesses. Lay your trust in them and step out of the way then you will be amazed at the results they can produce.

Focus on auto piloting: There are only two key elements to every business: Acquiring customers and talent. If you can autopilot both of them, your company is on "organic growth". Once this is done, your job shifts to identifying strategic boosters for your structure to make its giant steps.

Play to win not to lose: Now that you are not executing in your business and your company is on organic growth, you get a bird's eye view of your business and then you can identify what your business needs to win. Spend time updating yourself and becoming the best in your industry. Use the knowledge you acquire to provide insights into your business. Small insights and trivial course changes over time can have a big impact.

Setting up processes: If you extricate yourself from the day-to-day operations of one thing at a time, you will be completely free in a short period of time. Of course you can always take on new duties, but it should not be anything other than marketing and innovation. Your job is to set processes. Once the initiative becomes process driven or "operational", you can move out of it, handing it over to the next leader you identify.

As next steps, identify one thing that consumes most of your time in your business. Identify leaders on the team who can take it on. If there are none, look to hire one.

We all will agree that leadership is critical to the success of every venture, society, institution, and organization and even family.

Chapter 6: Breaking the rule in investments: What startups should know

From ideation to execution and growth can be really challenging to everyone especially if it is your first time venturing down the path of entrepreneurship. In this chapter, you will learn or realize some of the basics you have ignored so far that could actually contribute a great deal in moving you to the next level. For startups to be successful, they are basic hacks they must master in relation to finance and investments.

a) Master your financials

Your financials must be set straight from day one, if you do not have basic knowledge about financial management for example and cannot get someone on the board to assist you with this, it is important to outsource and learn the basics to enable you stay on track.

I am sure by now you should be wondering why it appears like being an entrepreneur means learning everything. The hard reality here is that not everyone from the start can afford a good board committed to their course. Usually from the idea stage, most people struggle alone to reach the level of an MVP. In this case, they have to wear many hates and become everything to their business. This is never an easy road but often times; people are more willing to join you on a course when they can see clearly what the end result will look like-in terms of product or service.

A lot of entrepreneurs have very great ideas and have a passion for the start-up they are working on. However, they always tend to overlook the one thing that would define the survival of their business – the finance aspect of it.

Entrepreneurs all get engrossed only with the financial aspect of how to raise capital for their business. This is an important aspect to pay attention. However, in paying attention to this aspect, you must not overlook the other aspect which is financial management. Come to think of it, if your start-up already has traction and needs to scale, the first and most important criteria that will give the investor second thoughts about your idea will be your financial statement. Yes, is all about finance, they are investing their money and want to know if they are handing it over to the right person. Therefore, know your financials if you want to succeed in entrepreneurship. Keep your accounting records clean.

There are different kinds of investors out there, some invest in the idea, others invest in the teams, and ultimately after they have invested their money, they would expect a return on their investment. The finance aspect I am referring to is the aspect that guarantees an investor a return and also that is the aspect that guarantees the success of your business.

Finance is not just debits and credits as we were once taught to believe. Things have evolved with time and today finance professionals are now seen as your partners in business because they are taught to use numbers to tell the story of a business from the beginning to the end. They are required to understand the make-up of every business so that every number tells a story.

The sad reality is that, most start-ups do not track or record their numbers. This is not because they know what to do and simply do not want to, it is rather because often times, the biggest issue is that most of them do not know what to track or what to record. In the end, we spend more time trying to repair what has been damaged or broken after some years or a period in business whereas we could have built a very solid foundation at the beginning.

"Different businesses need to record or track different things as every business is unique. Ultimately, the numbers would tell the same ending - a profit or a loss, a cash surplus or a cash deficit, a scale up or a shut down but the beauty in the way the numbers tell the story of the business is very different".

Remember this, after raising the much sought after investment capital and going through the stress of paper work and then sealing the deal, this is not all. Don't be deceived, that is just the beginning of a long journey.

From that time, the investor on a regular basis would expect to see your numbers. If you own a client based business, an investor would want to know how many new clients you have signed on, how many of them are regular customers, and how much you spend to acquire those customers.

Investors are not dumb, bear this in mind. They can quickly evaluate where a company is financially and this will influence their investment decision either positively or negatively.

The only prove that your business is sustainable is seen through the figures you present-the financial aspect, therefore if you must build a lasting business, start right away to put your records straight and every other thing will follow.

b) The responsibility to seek funds

If there is someone who masters a business more than any other person, it is the CEO. They master every single aspect of their business and therefore are in a better position to pitch it to an investor. Even though fund raising is not the sole responsibility of the CEO, they are the most qualified person strategically to handle this and get results. If you must raise the right funds for your startup, leave your comfort zone and get fully engaged in the process. Among all the things that can be delegated at an early stage in your startup, you cannot delegate this completely and still achieve expected results; except your product is so exceptional that it pulls investors to you instead of the other way round.

In the course of an interview with Mr. Ken Kengatharan, the Chairman and CEO of Auxesia Orion, these were his thoughts on the role a CEO should play regarding fund raising and management;

"I think there are three things that the CEO should be responsible for, one is making sure that the company is doing well financially; that is raising the capital. The other is investor relationship; which is related to the first. You need to have a good relationship with your investors, tell them how things are progressing.

Third is to be able to hire the right people at the senior level, make sure that the CEO is able to hire the right people. Now I do want to add a fourth one which I think is for technology based companies. It is valuable for the CEO to understand the technology inside out. I mean to start with, if you have to articulate the story to investors you have to know what you are talking about.

A great example of this is Elon Musk, even though he is the CEO of his company, he is involved in almost 60-80% of the technical aspect of the company then has a COO who is handling the entire business aspect. That will be the idea because I think in my opinion the visionary technologist has to be the CEO.

In most cases highly innovative companies that have to keep changing and evolving need to have a technology visionary leader as a CEO and then any business person as second in Command.

People have seen the effect of this in the way Apple has grown. At the beginning you had the founder, visionary and CEO when he was removed and some business people came in to run the company, it almost went bankrupt. Then the visionary founder came back and changed everything and the rest is history. I mean, this is one of the most valuable companies on the planet and when Steve jobs took over it was 90days from bankruptcy and that is the result of what happens when business people run companies and their focus is mainly return on investment to public investors who are often short term in many cases. Very few public investors especially in the United States are long term although there are long term investors but the majority unfortunately happens to be short term."

c) **Approaching investors, what startups should know**

Not every investor is the right fit for you or for your kind of venture or investment capital needed. This is because investors have specific preference. The two most important aspects you must consider are related to knowledge about the investor and knowledge about your startup. The next key thing is how to present it to an investor. Let's examine a few below:

i) Knowledge about the investor

Most investors prefer to invest in a field they master. In this case, it is important to research about an investor, and know in what sectors they are more likely to invest before approaching them.

Some investors besides having specific sectors of preference have specific geographic regions of interest, it is important to know this too before approaching them with your pitch.

Equally, some have specific stages of the startup they invest in. For example, an investor who prefers to invest at the seed stage might decide to focus all his investments at this level. It is important to know this before approaching them.

More to that, investors usually have personal motivations and affinities to specific subjects, areas, ideas, fields and even things and this sometimes could be as a result of their childhood experience or something that happened to them in the course of their life. In this case, they are

More interested in things that are related to these. In order to unlock a funding deal from them, one must be able to present to them something that matches their interest.

More importantly, Investors raise funds and anyone seeking funds should bare this in mind that the investment capital you are seeking from an investor at the end of the day may not be entirely theirs but that of a third party who has given them the responsibility to manage. They too therefore go through a hard time getting the deal sealed and you really do not expect them to give you venture capital when you haven't played your part. If you lose investment capital, you can raise it again from another source, but for an investor, this is like a vote of no confidence as they may not have a second chance. Therefore do not approach investors lightly and unprepared because they too have lots at stake to protect and investing in your venture is a logically calculated decision.

It is therefore critical to know an investor before approaching them so that you neither waste your time nor theirs and you can reduce the number of NOs you get which sometimes can be discouraging.

It is true most of the above apply to all investors no matter whether they are VCs, angel investors, equity investors or what have you. However, what applies to a VC might not apply to an angel investor. It is usually much more complicated when it comes to VC funding and many startups have gotten stocked at this level. For this reason, we have decided to go a step further with the topic.

ii) Approaching a venture capitalist: Getting their attention

I will not pretend to know the perfect solution view I am not a venture capitalist. In order to bring a comprehensive answer to the above, I decided to draw from a series of interviews conducted for this purpose. The first interviewee was of the opinion that,

- "The most important criteria to approach a VC is a perfect business plan. The business plan should be perfect, concise and much focused. In other words,
- Have a good business plan ready,

- Have a good team in place: Investors place a very high value on the team before taking any investment decisions
- Find a good mentor if possible
- Always remember entrepreneurs are very optimistic about their business but this might not be the case with an investor as perception and interest vary amongst different individuals

You must endeavor never to do the following

- Don't keep the pitch too lengthy. This is because investors go through several business plans in a day and might tend to lose interest if it is lengthy.
- Focus on your strength and what you have to offer not the other way round
- Don't be overly optimistic with financials. Be realistic as investors can easily call the bluff.
- Never ask for a non-disclosure agreement when you approach investors for the first time as this is a put off for the investor.
- Do not discuss valuations and equity stake with the investor during early stages."

The second interviewee advised,

"The core of all this is comfort; comfort of the investor, and to know that, they are placing their funds and reputation in people or teams that can deliver results. In many respects, if a VC does not do well, in one or more of the investments, they have a very hard time trying to raise money. If a venture capitalist doesn't do well they will not be able to raise the next money unlike an entrepreneur that can always start another company and look for other investors to invest in. So in this case it comes down to how much comfort the VC has in the field of investment. Just because you have a great technology does not guarantee you will get the investments.

Remember that these are long term investments; some of these investments from investment phase to exit are longer than marriages; which also means relationship. Think about this yourself, if you as an individual want to put money in something, you will be very careful to the point that you also want to know that the person you are dealing with is someone you are familiar with.

One way to make sure that you get their attention is to make sure that you know someone who knows you well that that particular venture capitalist also knows. I will say that is the number one way to get the Venture capitalist attention.

Secondly, you have to fit into the investment pieces of the Venture capitalist that is, not all venture capitalist is looking for a quick return and so they will invest in anything they see. No, they are specialized, sometimes along industries, sometimes along stages of investment, and even specialized along how long they can hold their investments so that is another one.

Then you have to bring it down to the partner, at the end of the day is the partner who is the internal champion who has to push through the argument among other partners and they are all investors and limited partners. And so a background on the partner to make sure that that person will understand what it is you are trying to do is the key. Coming from a similar background makes life easy. You don't want to spend 9months trying to educate somebody on what the underlying technology is. You want to make sure that the underlying story is already understood by the VC.

I think a perfect point to enter and get VCs to like your story and immediately go for investment is, if you are one of the three or five companies within a specific space, and that at the time it is hot, if a particular VC had missed out on a particular investment opportunity, especially if they had spent a long time looking unto the background of the story, the opportunity etc., then that's the best because they would have done all the background work and you walking up to them with a similar solution that they missed out on becomes a very fast investment. In which case, you can go from an introduction to closing within weeks or a couple of months.

Bottom line, it is very much a people business and for that you have to make sure you have done a lot of research on the VC that you want to touch and in this respect, you really do not want to be as somebody who is sending a business plan to everybody and no one.

Nobody likes to be paddling a village bicycle basically, they will want to feel that they are exclusive and that you are watching them because there is a fit and that you are not presenting this to anybody else.

He added that, some people compare entrepreneurs finding VCs to someone going on a blind date to find their life partner. It is very much like that. This is about a partnership for a long term and so if

you really don't know your investor, and try to understand what they are thinking and what's important to them, then there is no partnership and whether it be marriage or a business relationship, you cannot understand what everybody is trying to achieve in their own world and whatever you are proposing is not a solution for everybody to benefit from then this is not going to work.

A lot of the times, I can tell you that the benefits are not necessarily monetary which means you are not looking for how many x multiples that you can get in terms of the dollar. A lot of times is intangible, one of the examples could be that a particular VC or investor is interested in putting money in coming up with a new drug for a certain disease because maybe their parents are suffering from it or they died of it or they know somebody who has had that. If it is country specific, it may be someone who feels they want to give back to their own community, country or people. Therefore you need to understand what they want and their motivation if you want to succeed with them.

A majority of the time, you cannot get this on email alone, you need to meet them in person to understand otherwise people won't tell you the real reasons on phone or by email. You need to meet them in person and you need to make that happen.

I have heard this many times where the investor says if the entrepreneur is not willing to go the extra mile to find ways to make it happen, it will be difficult for them to know whether or not if they invest in this person, they will go the extra mile to make the venture succeed.

This therefore means that, a majority of the times people are trying to interpret your actions and understand how that could be like when the investment is made.

Therefore you have to be careful about this if you are working to attract a Venture capitalist

So knowing your investor in this case is extremely important than finding the money at times because lots of entrepreneurs don't do this, you should follow one person at a time, in fact 80% of the time you should do the research on an investor and make sure that you understand where they are coming from and only 20% should be the pitch and you should not be sending your business plan or anything to anyone you feel doesn't have a fit. Just like investors are being selective on the entrepreneurs, the entrepreneurs have to be selective on the investors. It's both ways.

iii) Think long term while accepting investment capital

This is another key thing entrepreneurs must note. Like we have mentioned above, there are various categories of investors. You have the venture capitalist which is the traditional one then you have others like cross over investors and hedge funds amongst others. These have more short term requirements because that is what those investors have promised to their own investors as to how their money will be deployed. In which case they have partners and fund managers but they have their own investors, limited partners or otherwise.

If any has said, *"our investor thesis is we put money in and take money out, in 6mounths time or 9months time,"* that's their thesis and the way they are working. In many respects, these venture funds and large companies take a portfolio approach to how they employ their capital because you don't want to give in all the money to a venture capitalist or an investor who doesn't do it the same way.

It is therefore important to identify the long term thinking investors because some do think long term, even beyond 10years and others because of the way the fund is structured.

They are other investors who are called evergreen with whom there is no set time that they have to return on the investments. Many of these are investment groups out of large companies.

It is important to note that, long term is important because it shows dedication from the entrepreneur to stay the course until the return is made and that's what the investors are looking for. The old adage is, you don't build something for sale. If you are building something for sale, you won't have many buyers out there. If people like what you are building, then they will come and buy you along the way.

So you should not be thinking of, "I will build this and then I will go public for a number of years and I will sell everything. That should be secondary, you should be thinking about building something that will last and if another company likes what you have and they come in and want to buy you then you sell the company after talking to the investors who put money in your company.

So thinking long term is very important because it also means that you can be competitive because someone will produce something similar if they like what you are doing and unless you are thinking long term, you will be out of the market and you won't be able to survive(Ken Kengatharan)

Knowledge about your startup

If you want to achieve greater success with investors, you must have your business in the right order as discussed in the previous chapters and you must also have your documents in place. Don't let an investor teach you how to build a pitch deck, he obviously does not have the time to do that. Make your pitch as clear and comprehensive as possible; also mind the length of your pitch as few people will have the time to read through a lengthy pitch.

Mastering all these may not be a solution to all your funding problems but will serve as part of the solution. Everything being equal, your chances will be increase.

Chapter 7: Networking

i) Mastering the rules

Everyone wants to build the right network and surround themselves with the right people to assist them in one way or the other to achieve their objectives. Some people have taken time to master the Dos and Don'ts of networking while others have not. What I will advise is that you read all the important material you can find on networking, ask questions from successful people and do what it takes to get the right results.

I will limit myself to a few things you should avoid doing when networking with people, you can add to the list to create your networking guidelines. Below are a few:

Address people properly: I get quite a good number of messages on LinkedIn from connections which often start with "how are you my friend?" and I am like wow, for real?

This doesn't at all appear offensive in any way at first view, but from my experience and those of others I have followed closely, connections like this are more likely to be ignored. But come to think of it, how do you call someone you are just connecting with virtually for the first time my friend?

I don't know about you but this always appears to me as being overly disrespectful especially when you really do not know anything about the person, the truth is that most in my case end up turning the professional relationship into some social media scenario where it becomes a story of how much they had fallen in love with you. This is what I do, from the moment I receive this, I take the necessary action to ensure no one's time is wasted.

Be honest: Some persons you know very well have the kind of profile online you stumble on and you are surprise. Nothing they write about themselves is true. I admire the fact that we love to be important, at least take time to work for it and to deserve it because most people before taking a business relationship to the next level will do their background checks and when they discover this about you, the wrong recommendations start going out,

I personally received a connection request sometime last year that got me really upset. Someone I personally knew had a bio that was stronger than that of my most experienced connection. They presented themselves as expert in so many things I personally know they have no idea in. Remember, the connections you create are important, but when someone recommends you or introduces you to another person it create even a more impactful relationship. Make sure you are the kind of connection people will want to recommend.

Don't stalk people: No one wants to receive inappropriate content from you in their mailbox the next day once they hit accept on your connection request on social; they will simply mark you as spam.

No one wants you calling them on what Sapp at your convenience without prior notification; they might be in an important business meeting. No one wants your prying into their privacy without permission.

Don't ask obvious questions: By obvious questions here I mean questions you could easily find answers to by visiting the person's profile or by carrying out some research about them prior to establishing contact.

Questions like;

<u>What is your name?</u>

<u>Where do you live?</u>

<u>Where do you work?</u>

Are turnoffs at first contact especially when you connect with someone on a platform like LinkedIn where you can easily find these answers just by glancing through their profile introduction. This is because these fields are mostly obligatory on LinkedIn profile settings and therefore everyone who has a LinkedIn profile must have that.

When you inbox a connection for the first time with these turnoff questions, it already puts you at a default position in their mind and in most cases, they are bound to go cold on you. It is true you will always stumble on people who never reply to inbox messages on such platforms even without these questions. But avoiding them will increase your chances of building meaningful relationships with those you succeed to communicate with in the right way.

Don't ask for endless favors from contacts: You don't just want to keep asking one favor after another from your contacts else you make the relationship overly burdensome. Sometimes offer to assist them too in something and don't just remain on the receiving end.

ii) Building confidence

Relationships are just like startups, they take time to grow. You need to feed them, nurture them and watch them mature. Value your network and invest in building confidence every step of the way. People will only go a step further with you if they can trust you.

iii) Keep in touch

Often times managing your ever growing network is tricky with our schedule that grows more and more each day. If you want to have the best out of your network, treat it like an investment, even better, treat it like part of your task each day-keep in touch with your valued connections and always find time to make them feel your presence once in a while. What happens often is that, while you are trying to expand your network, they too are working just as hard to expand theirs. They meet new people and are constantly doing so. Therefore, giving your relationship with each person in your network some more value helps them to stay conscious you are valuable and can open other doors for you.

iv) Stay keen to opportunities that show up

This is where you benefit from your network. After taking time to progressively move from the level of networking to a working relationship, after building the confidence required for any business dealings to pull through smoothly, it is time to benefit from the process. Most

Opportunities will not come directly to you, you will need to create some, someone will have to recommend you for some and others you need to be keen enough to notice them and exploit them. All in all, learn to be proactive even at this level and do your best to embrace opportunities that are favorable to you.

v) Building your online profile

In this era where automation and online presence have become key aspects of every business, it is important to understand what platforms work best for you and concentrate your efforts in ensuring your brand stands out. This sometimes might be costly especially for startups with little capital trying to launch their products on the market for the first time but you really don't have to do this all at once.

You can decide to build your personal brand first and then your product brand. What is important here is that, every founder is the first brand ambassador of their product and therefore if your personal brand stands out well, chances are your product brand will follow automatically. I mean, this is the only reason companies hire public figures as brand ambassadors or pay them high to advertise their products. Therefore, chose rightly and make sure you exploit the opportunities at your disposal to grow your brand and stand out. In other to achieve this, we will focus on LinkedIn and personal branding in the subsequent paragraphs

a) LinkedIn

You will be surprise how many leads people in the same field like you have generated from LinkedIn without paying a cent. Though this is really not all about leads, there is a lot you can get from LinkedIn with an up to date and professional profile.

Personally, I will not be able to do what I do today successfully without LinkedIn, not even sure i would be able to write this book without all the wonderful people I met on LinkedIn, connected with, bonded with and even partnered and collaborated with some.

This is what I will advise:

Your profile picture: Your profile picture is as important as your name. It feels weird when someone receives an invitation to connect from you and you have no profile picture. It feels even

More absurd when they notice you already have over 100 connections. The question that comes to mind is: how did they know this person?

If you must get connections that matter on LinkedIn and that are out of your physical network, you must have a profile picture, not just any, but one that appears professional.

Title: When someone receives a request and it appears: N N

No one has the patience to go through your profile to find out what you do.

Equally, if you left the university 5 years ago, you cannot still have your title today as

Attended University of…

It is easy for someone who originally does not know you to ignore your request and move on.

Your summary: It is another important part; you must make sure you write a summary that focuses on the exact thing you will want people to know you for. Let this section carry a few of your greatest achievements in your field; you could add up to five or six maximum just so it does not look too lengthy. It should actually be a summary and not your entire resume because you will have an opportunity to present your working experience right after that. Whether you are generating leads, job hunting or networking, it is important to keep your target reader at the back of your mind while crafting this part of the profile.

You must constantly think of ways to make their lives easier and what you will want them to take away as message after visiting your page. Make your headline stand out by listing your specialty and speaking directly to your audience. Thanks to free SEO tools available online, you can now check and include searchable keywords in this section of the profile while making sure it remains within a 10 words limit.

Then take note of all what you could add to make your profile look real. For example, videos, links to your websites, documents, pictures etc.

Working experience: your working experience, you want to make sure that when someone visits your profile they do not just see studied in or worked in and that is the end.

Take time to fill out your educational background and your working experience or volunteering experience; in case you have no working experience. Pay attention to details in all these parts as this is what represents you online to other professionals who do not know you physically.

Try to fill out information in all the section. Include skills and volunteering experience then you can add every other thing that doesn't fit in your introduction but can go in this section jut to ensure your profile looks real. This doesn't mean you should fill in all you ever did even if it's not relevant to your present career. Instead, select those that are relevant to your career goals and add them to your profile.

The other important aspect is to ask for recommendations from people that know you personally and have worked with you, it could be your employer, manager, colleague, supervisor etc. This gives you an extra credibility and people will tend to trust you more when they connect with you especially if they know the person(s) that recommended you.

Now if you are looking to make something meaningful out of your time invested on LinkedIn, you must be willing to take further steps. Here, we will draw a lot from the works of previous authors on the same subject.

Leads generation

Leads generation, just like every marketing strategy requires basic mastery. To be able to get the right leads for your business, you must first identify your target market. By so doing the category of people you will like to target. Then you must identify where to find them.

On LinkedIn, their search key words have made this much more easier as you can type in the name of a particular group e.g. HR and LinkedIn algorithm will be able to direct you to people with these key word on their profile.

Now not every search result is your target, someone might just appear on your search results because they had used your key word some time on a post or article. You then have to be able to select to make sure that you are getting the right people for your business. That way you will avoid wasting your time and that of your contacts.

After narrowing down to the target, you can then continue with the next phase. Truth be told, not everyone you will target will end up being a client, you must bare this in mind. Yes they are the category of people you are looking for, but you also have to find out if your solution resolves their problem.

A typical example of this we have looked at above is when you are looking for investors. You will realize they are many investors and you can find them everywhere. However, not all investors will be interested in your solution especially because of their area of preference which could also be driven by so many underlying reasons you ignore. If you approach the right investor with the wrong business idea, he automatically becomes a wrong investor for you.

So leads generation in itself is an art which must be studied and practiced gradually, then mastered in order to succeed.

Conclusion - Thrive

In most societies, it is not easy to be an entrepreneur especially because people around you have difficulties understanding why you will have to consciously engage in a venture you know will only bring in returns after many years; that's in a case where it is successful. People have had to wait for 10years or more to reach breakeven in there ventures. Now this is a hard reality to accept especially in less advanced economies with high levels of poverty and large family sizes. This has made the journey even more difficult for people with such realities who sometimes have given up.

A few weeks back I had a conversation with someone in the space who shared his experience on the subject. he had told me he has visited quite a good number of incubators in his countryy and the hard reality was that, each time he noticed the number of young people frequenting the space kept on reducing and from this, I came to the conclusion that, there was the absence of a support system making it impossible for young people to pursue their entrepreneurial dreams especially in countries in Africa with a weak or inexistent startup/ entrepreneurial ecosystem.

Your journey as an entrepreneur will not be an easy one but will be worth it. Work always with the mindset of success and when failure comes, learn from it and move to the next level. Do not plan to fail but plan to succeed and use every opportunity you find worthy to move closer towards success.

www.ingramcontent.com/pod-product-compliance
Lightning Source LLC
Chambersburg PA
CBHW021512210526
45463CB00002B/990